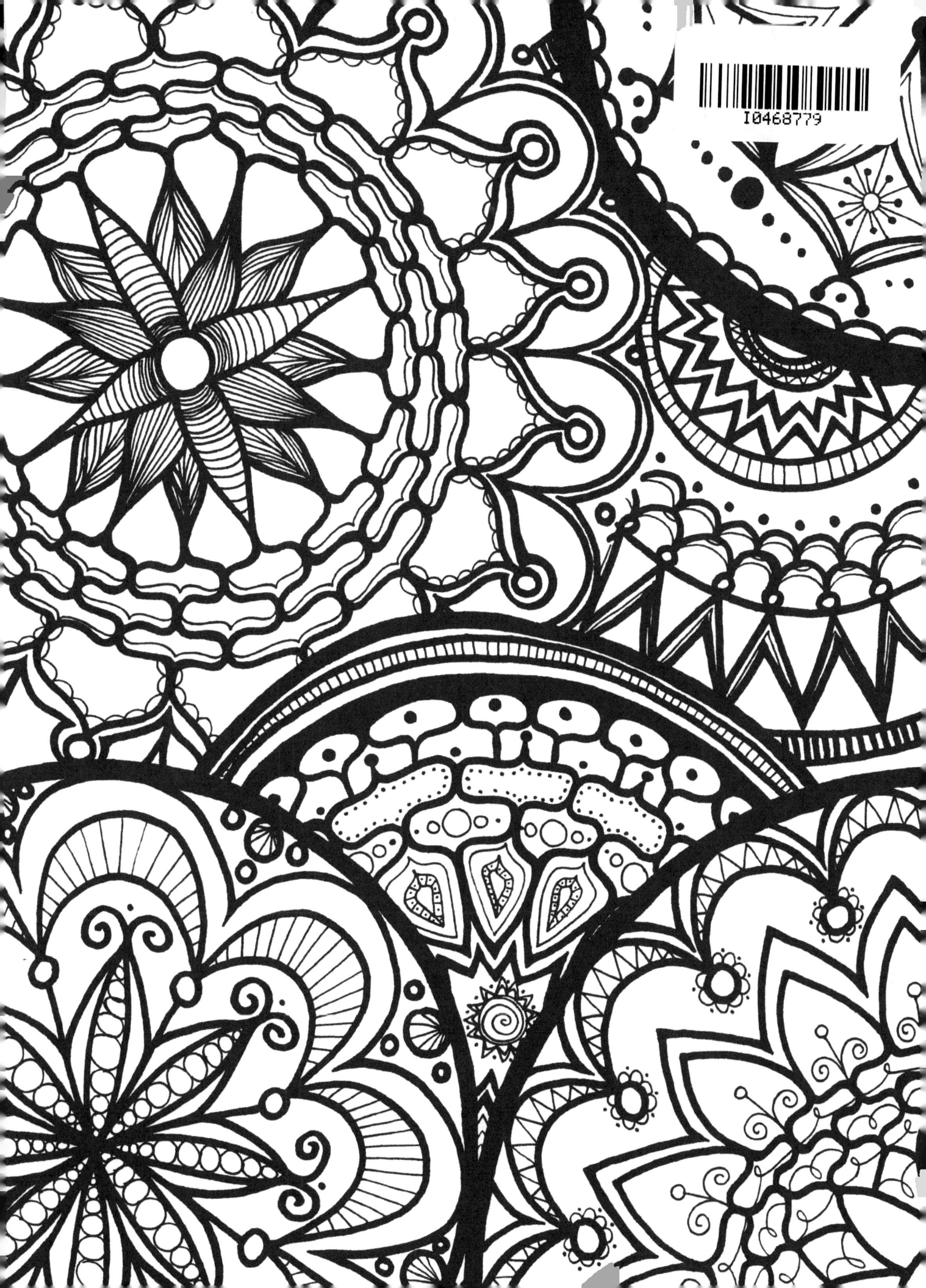

Colored by:

_____

SarahMe Doodles

by Sarah K. Presslor

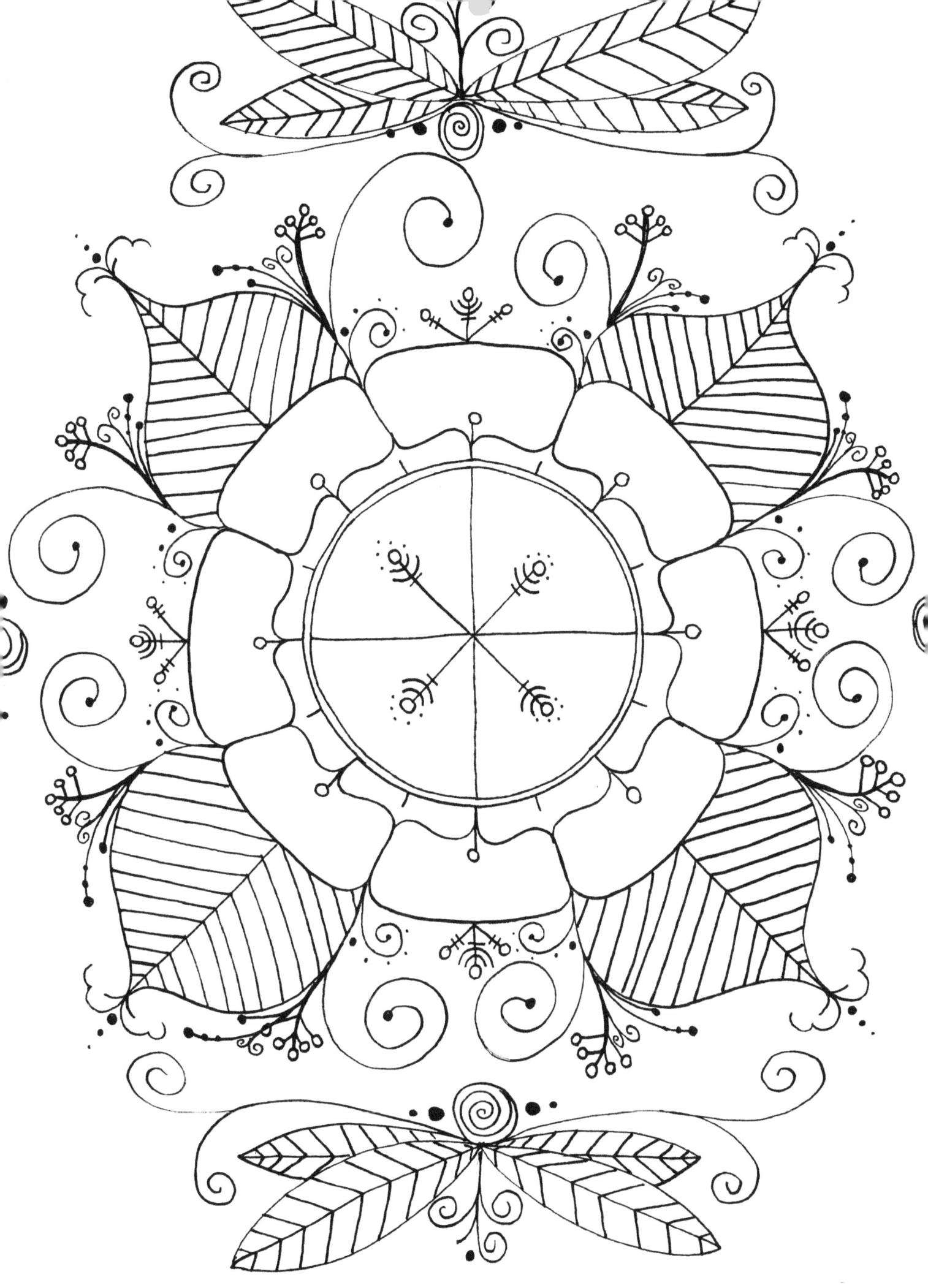

Colored by:

_____

SarahMe Doodles
by Sarah K. Presslor

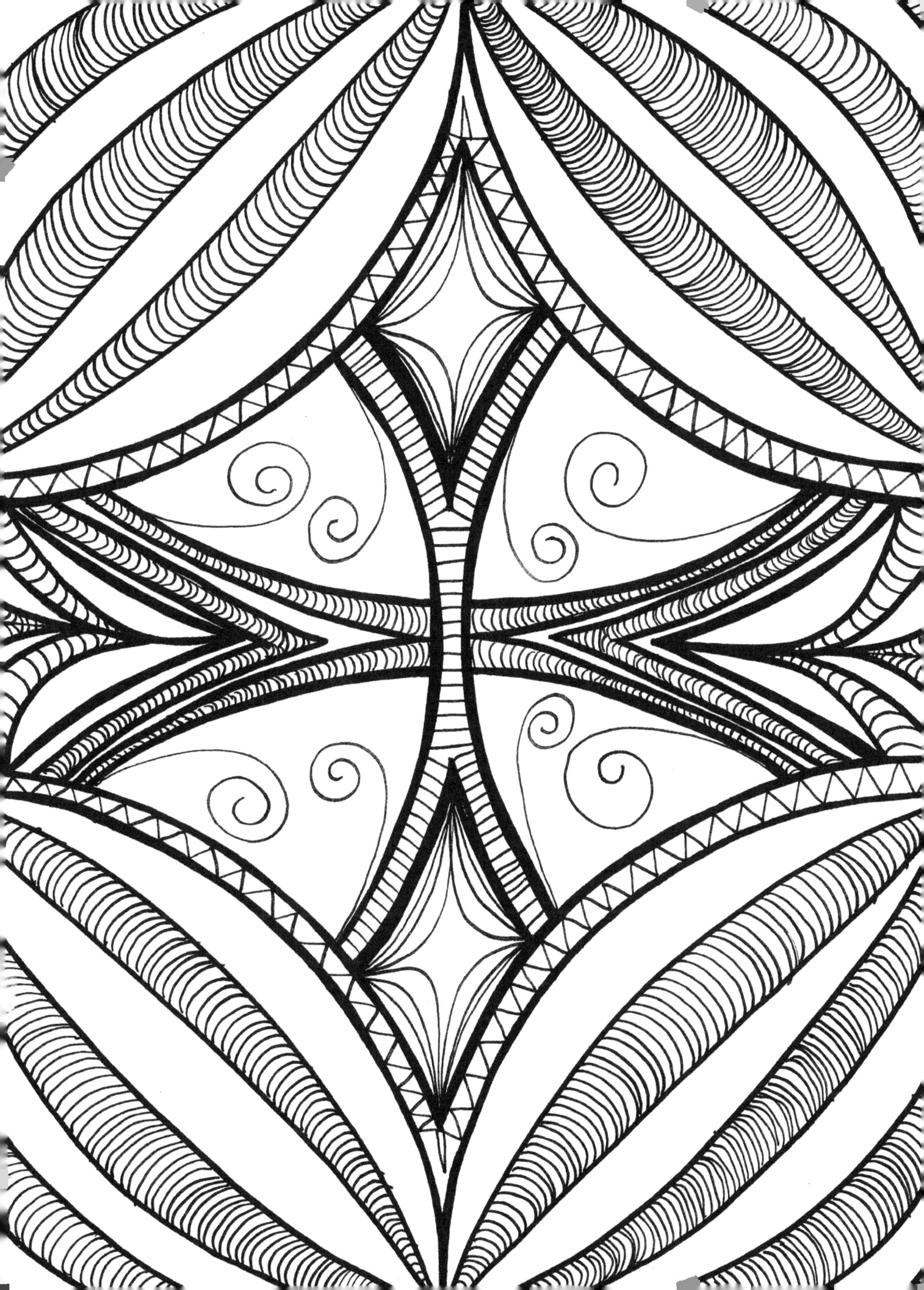

Colored by:

_____

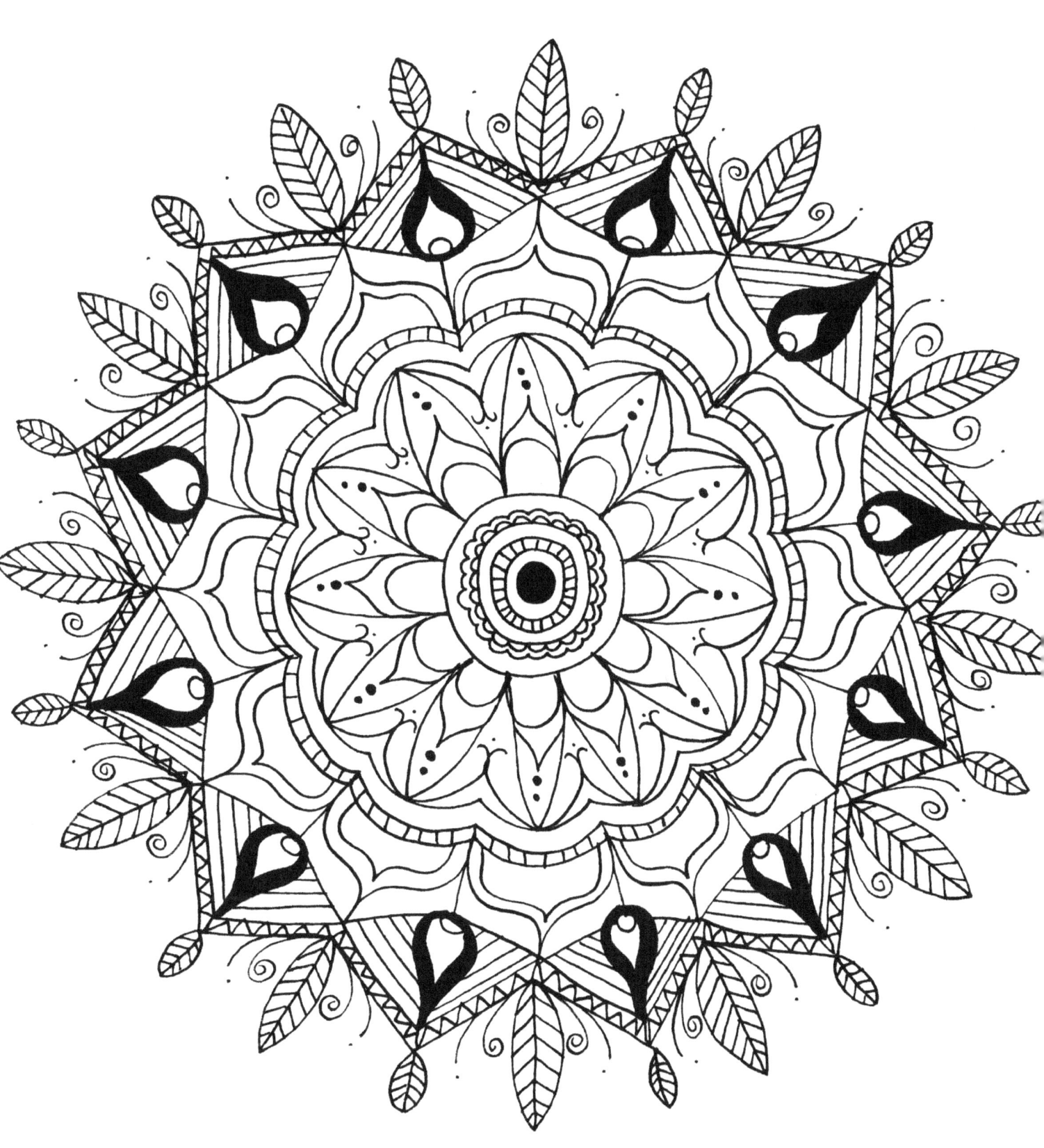

Colored by:

_____

SarahMe Doodles

by Sarah K. Presslor

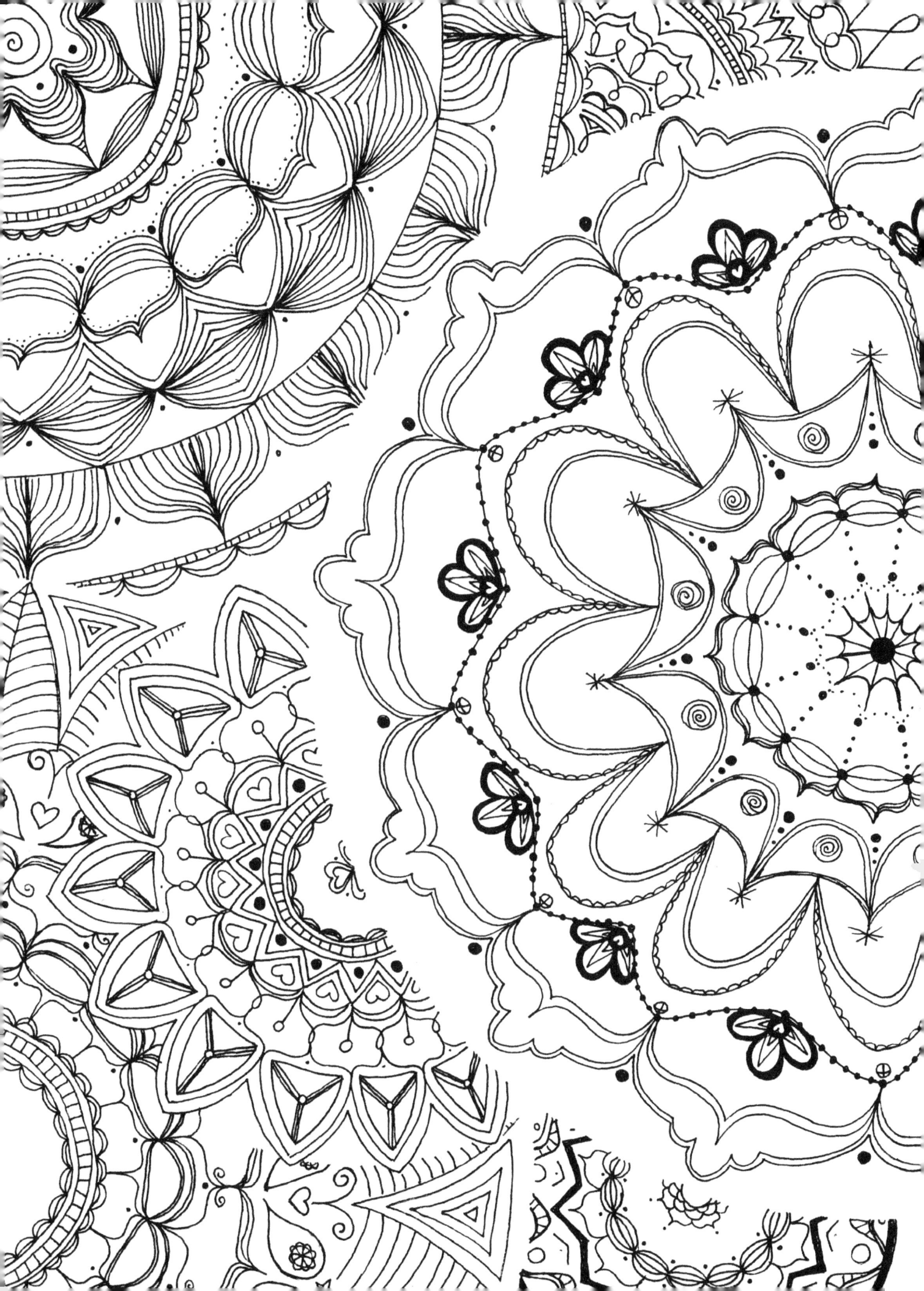

Colored by:

_____

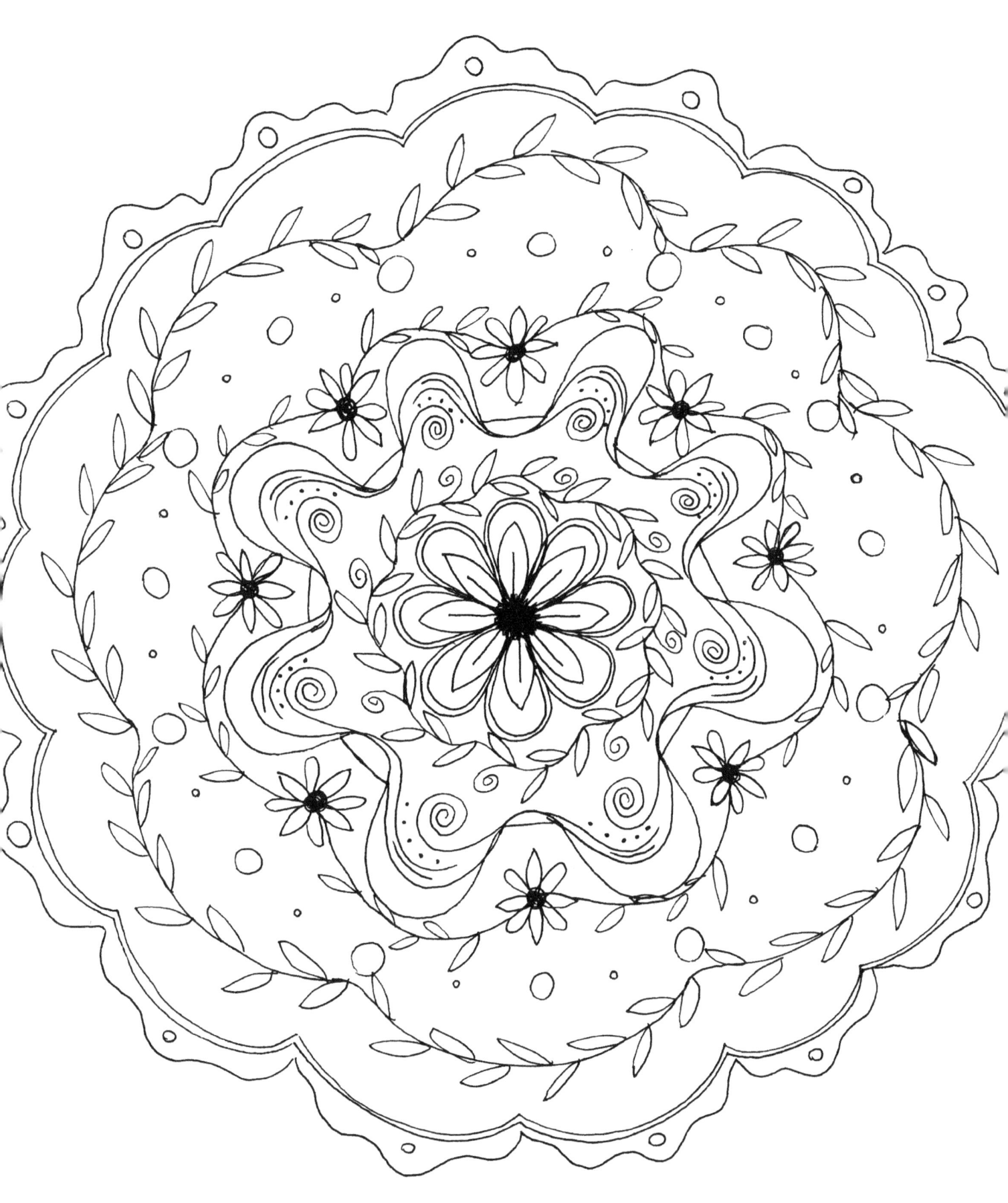

Colored by:

_____

SarahMe Doodles

by Sarah K. Presslor

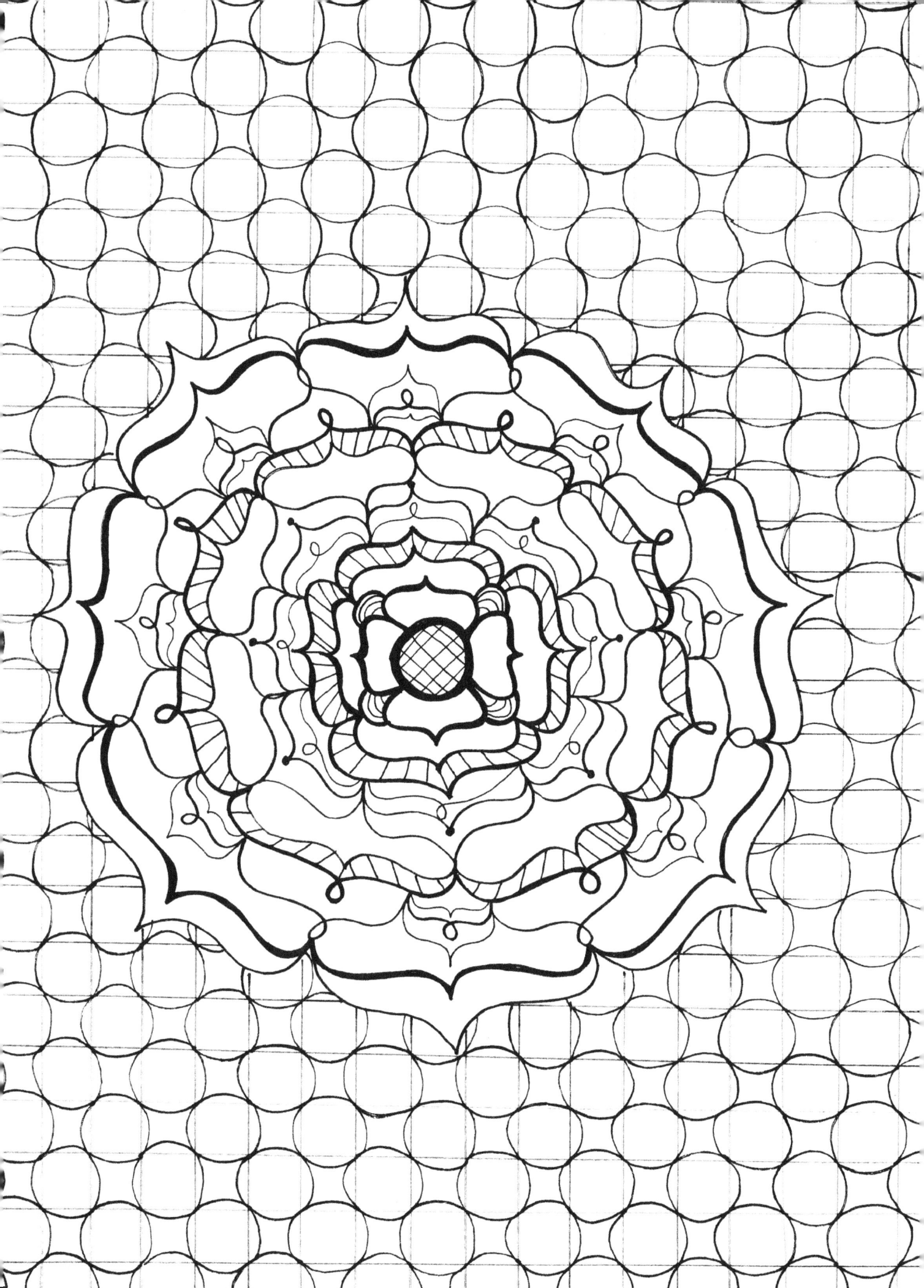

Colored by:

_____

SarahMe Doodles

by Sarah K. Presslor

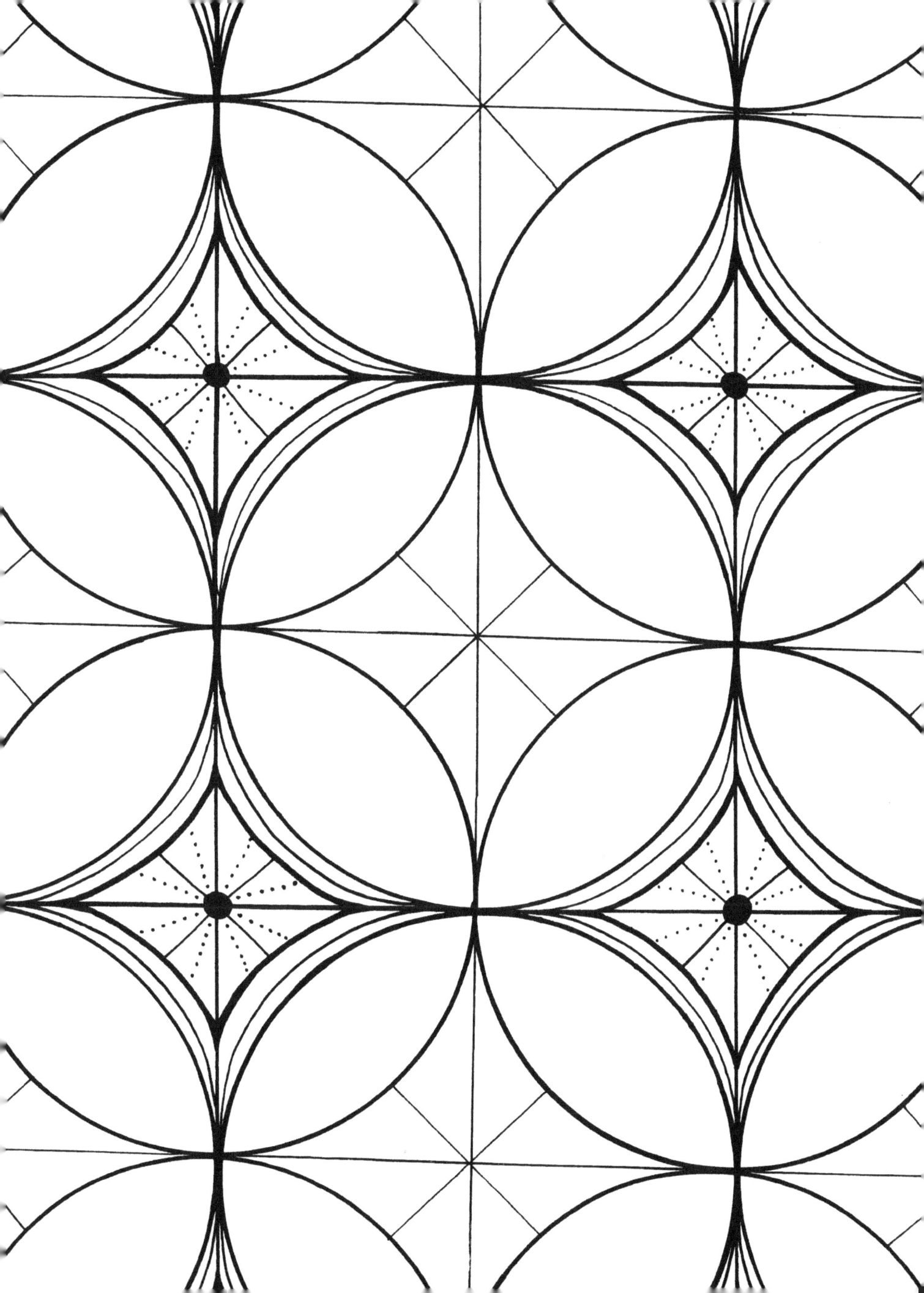

Colored by:

_____

SarahMe Doodles

by Sarah K. Presslor

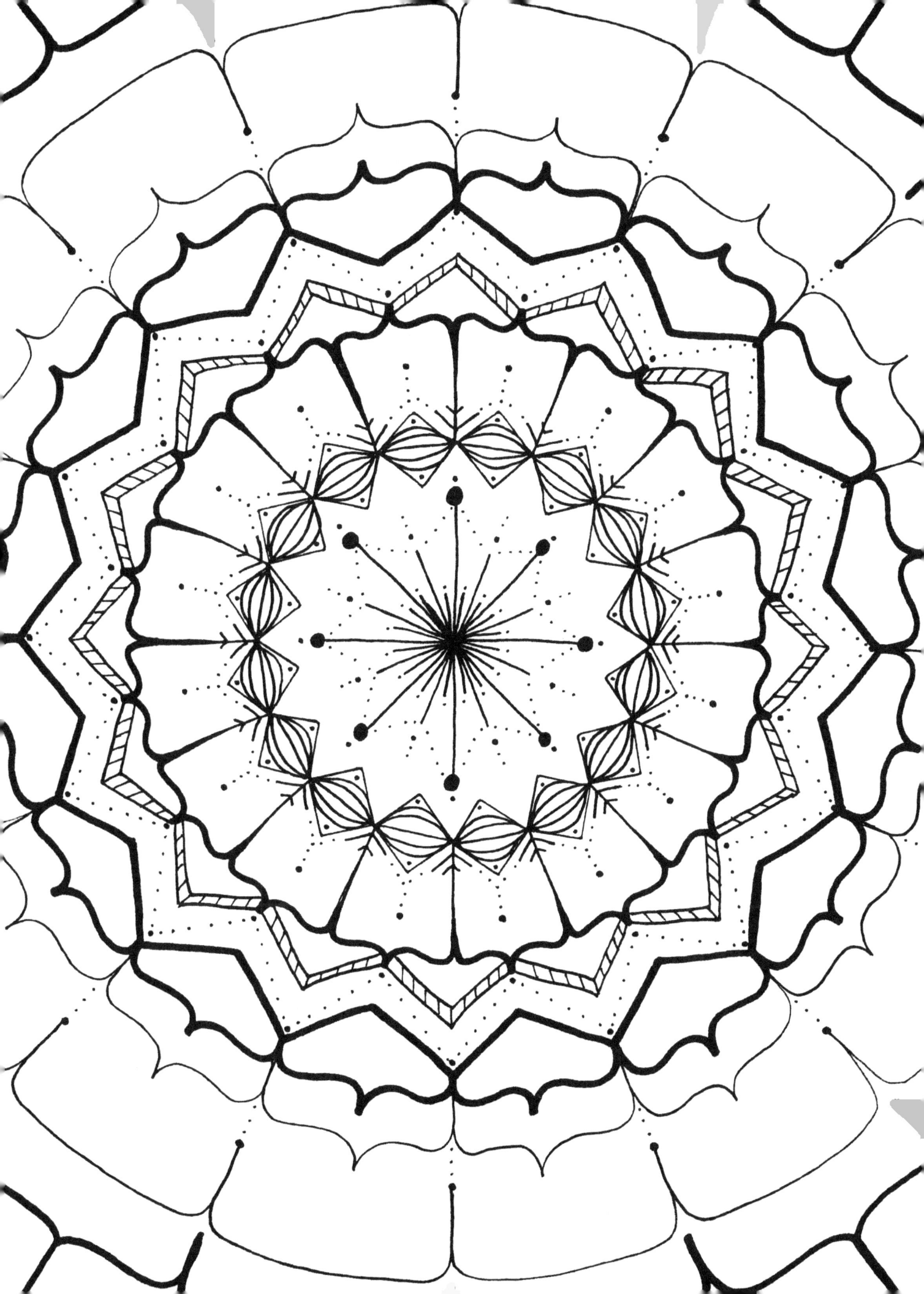

Colored by:

_____

SarahMe Doodles

by Sarah K. Presslor

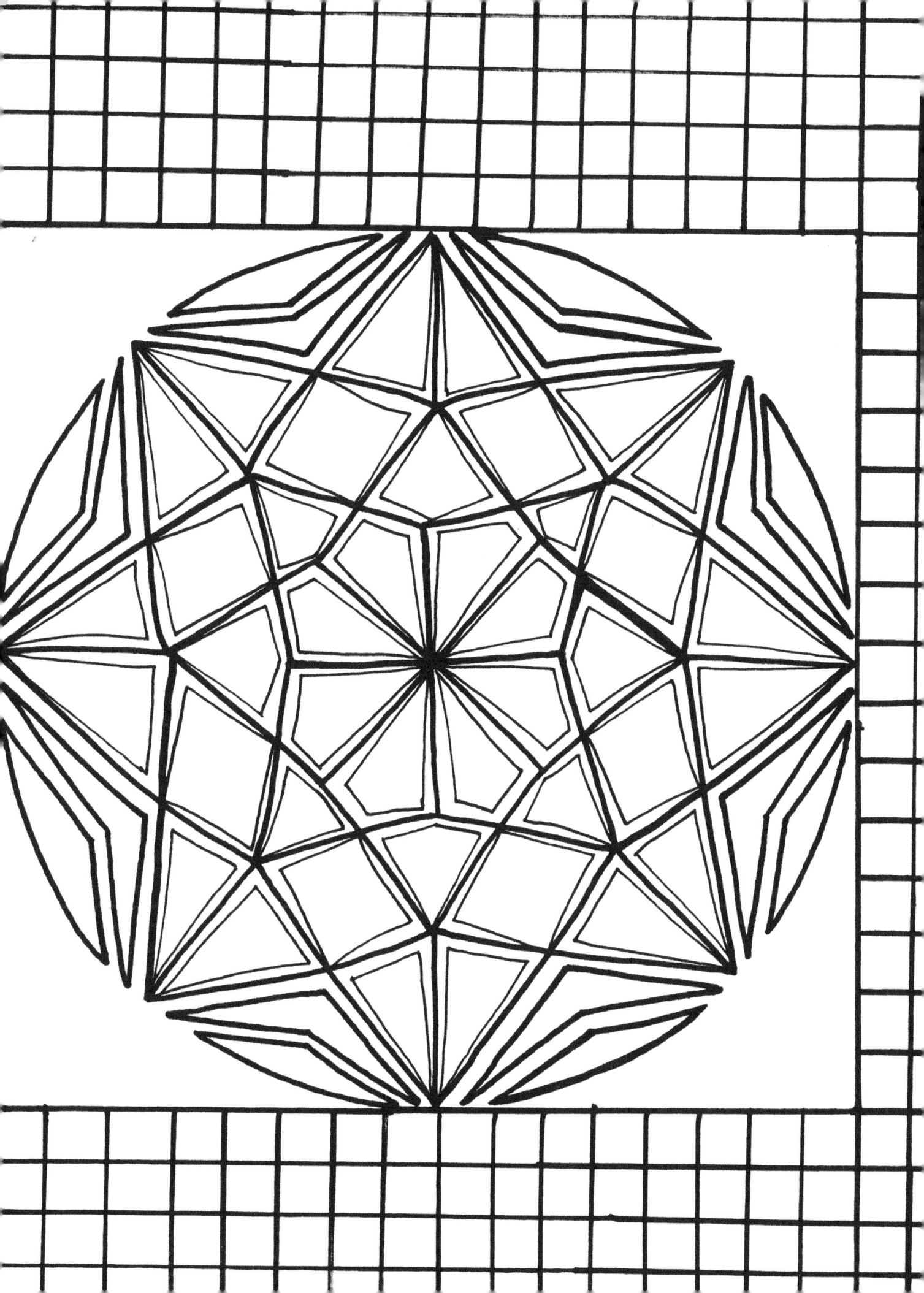

Colored by:

_____

SarahMe Doodles
by Sarah K. Presslor

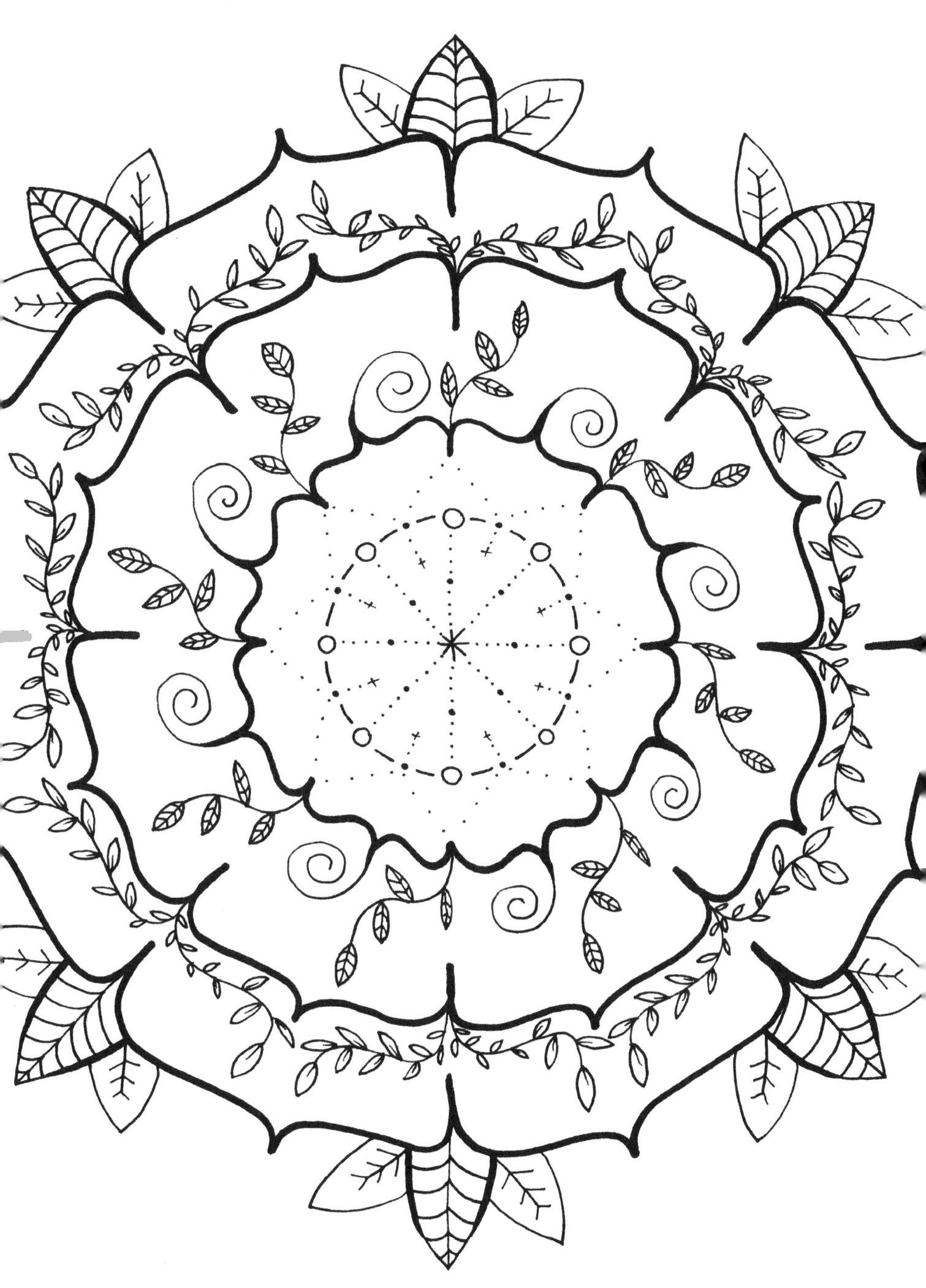

Colored by:

_____

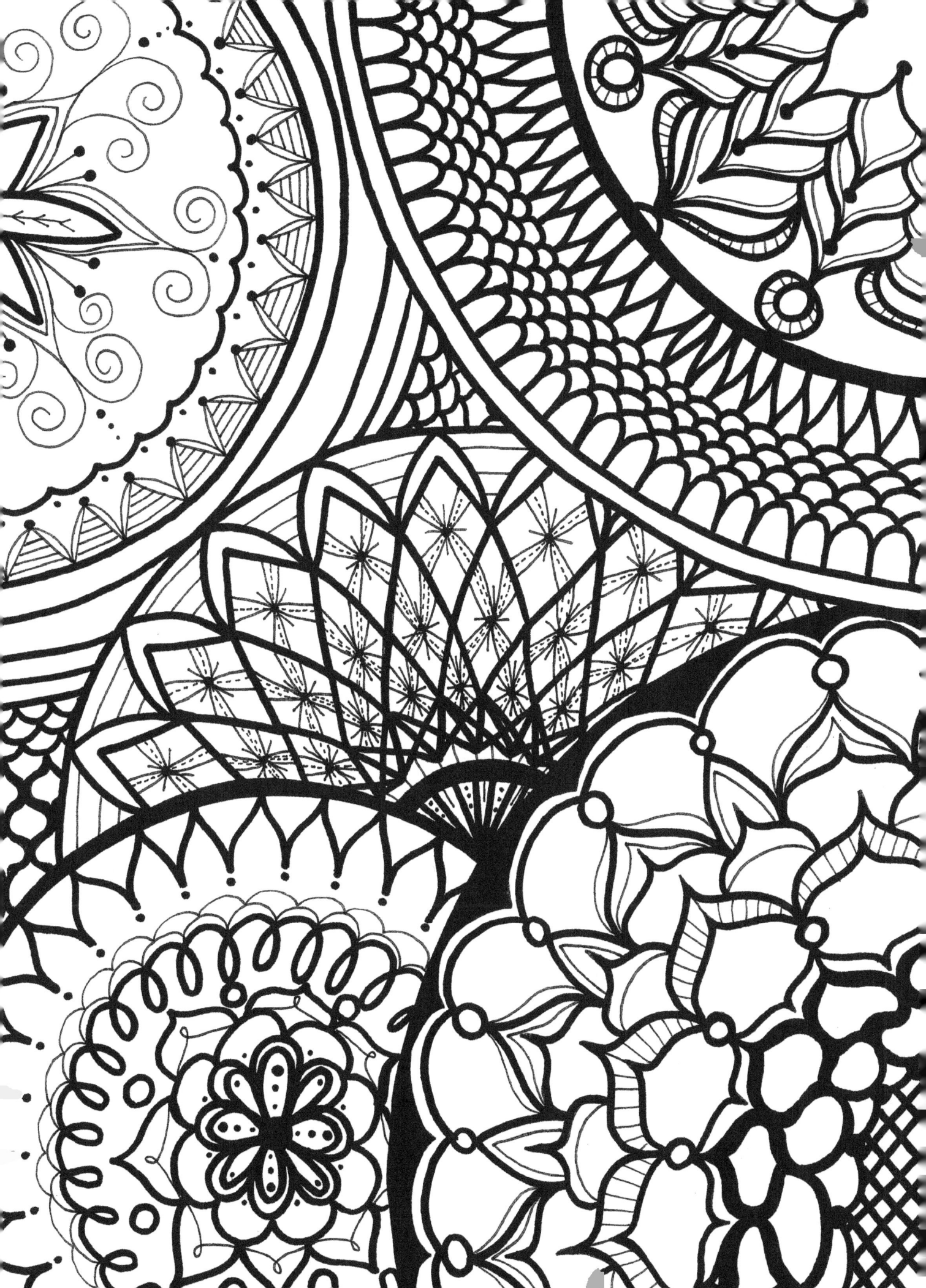

Colored by:

_____

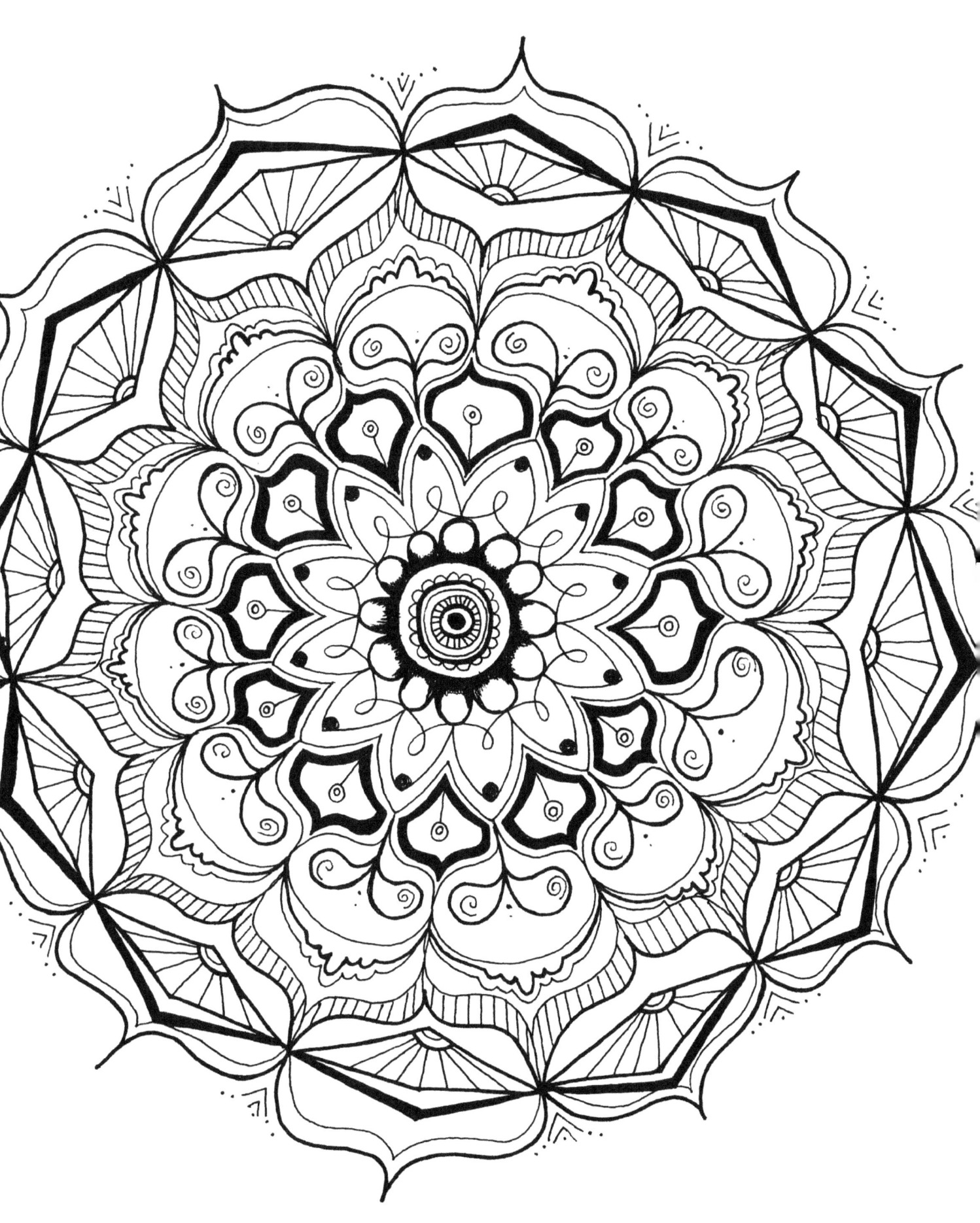

Colored by:

_____

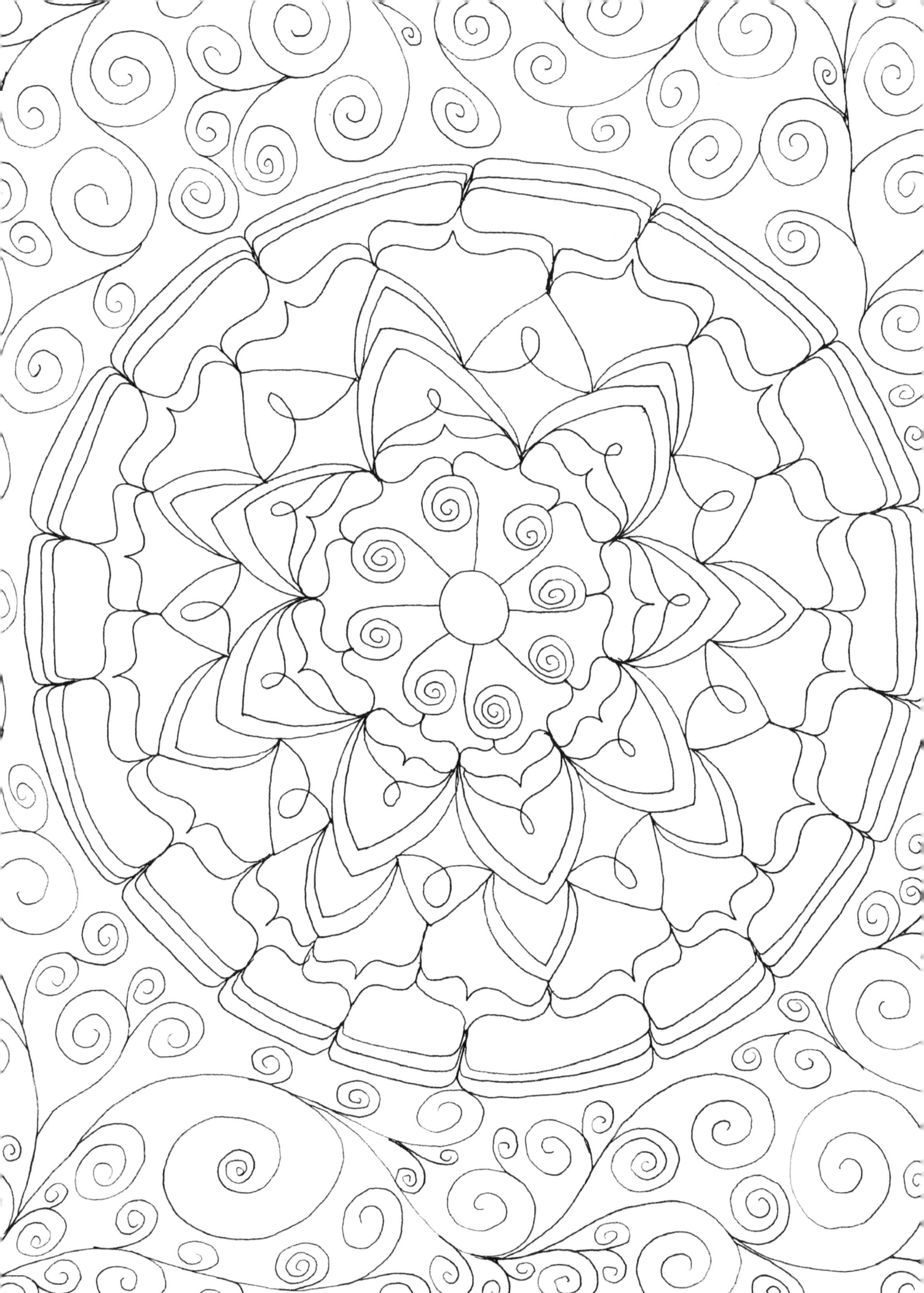

Colored by:

_____

SarahMe Doodles
by Sarah K. Presslor

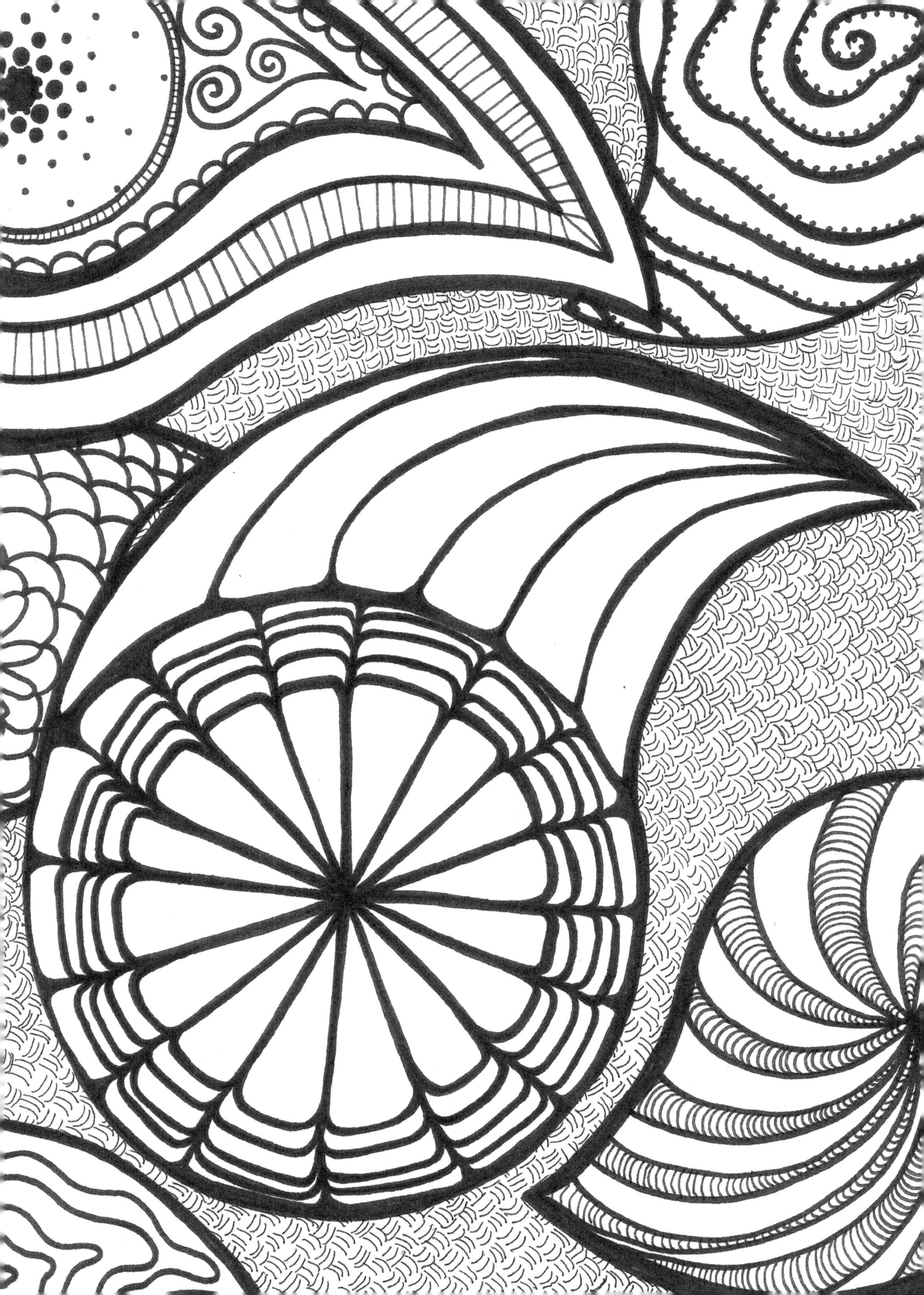

Colored by:

_____

SarahMe Doodles

by Sarah K. Presslor

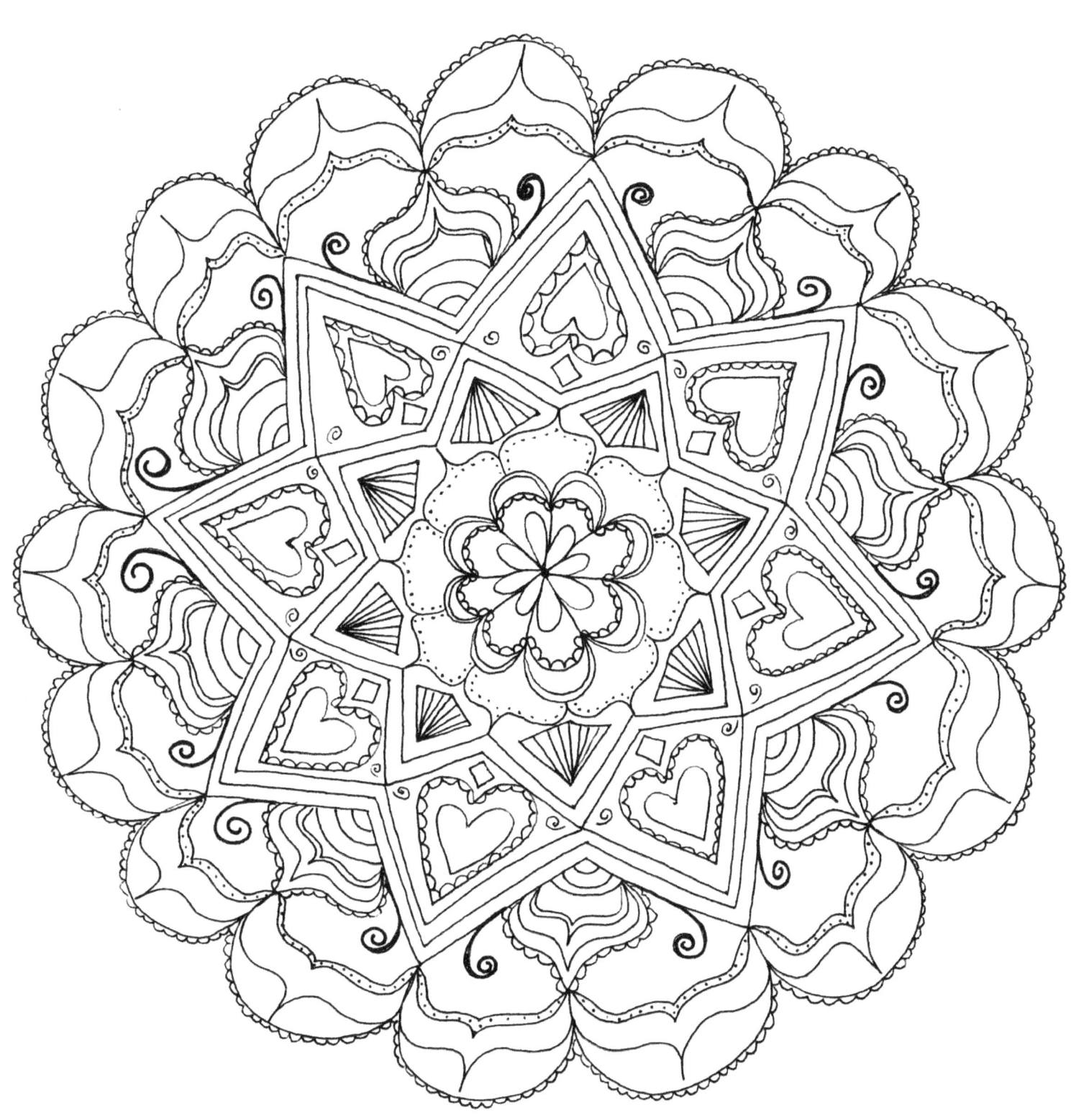

Colored by:

_____

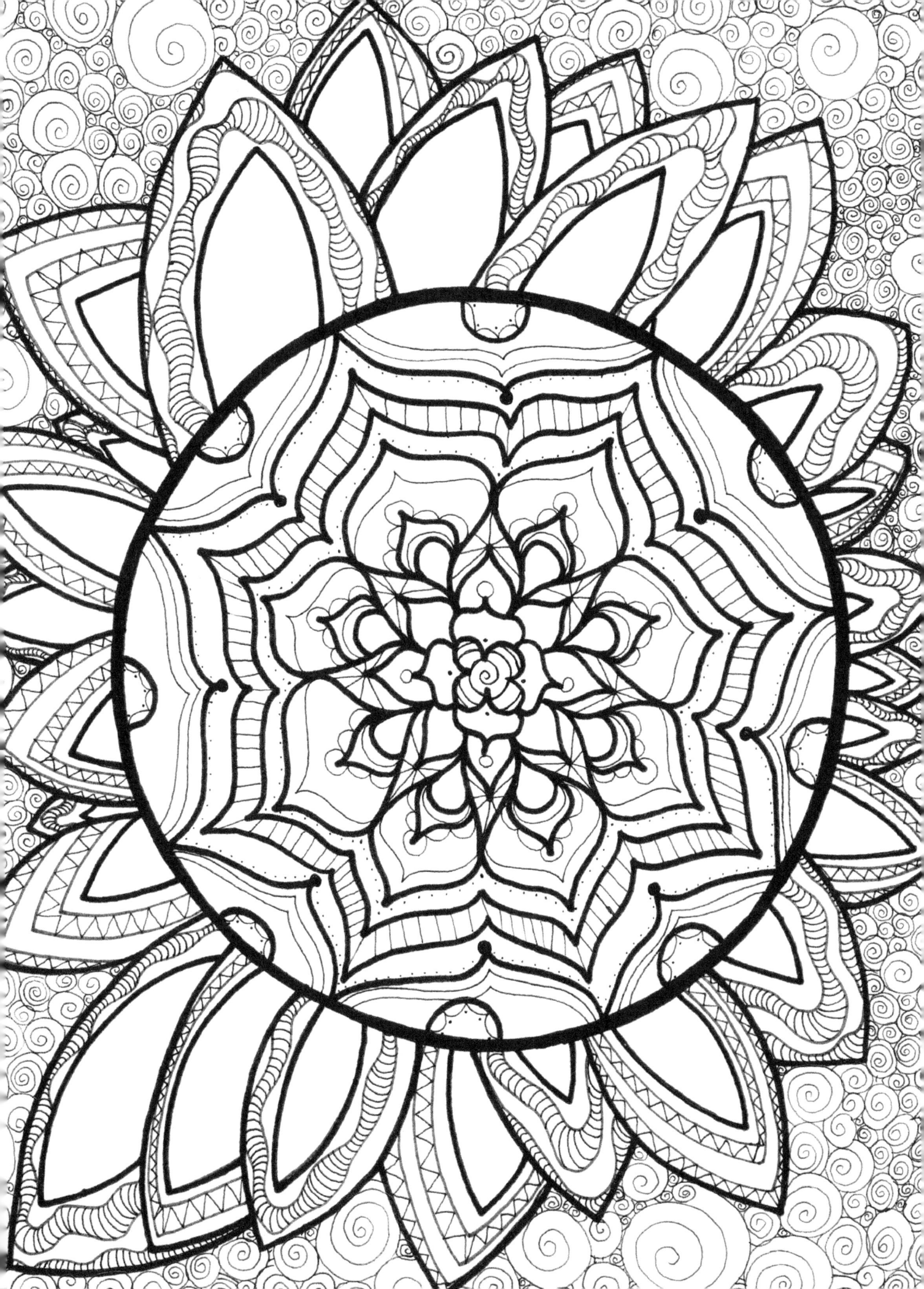

Colored by:

_____

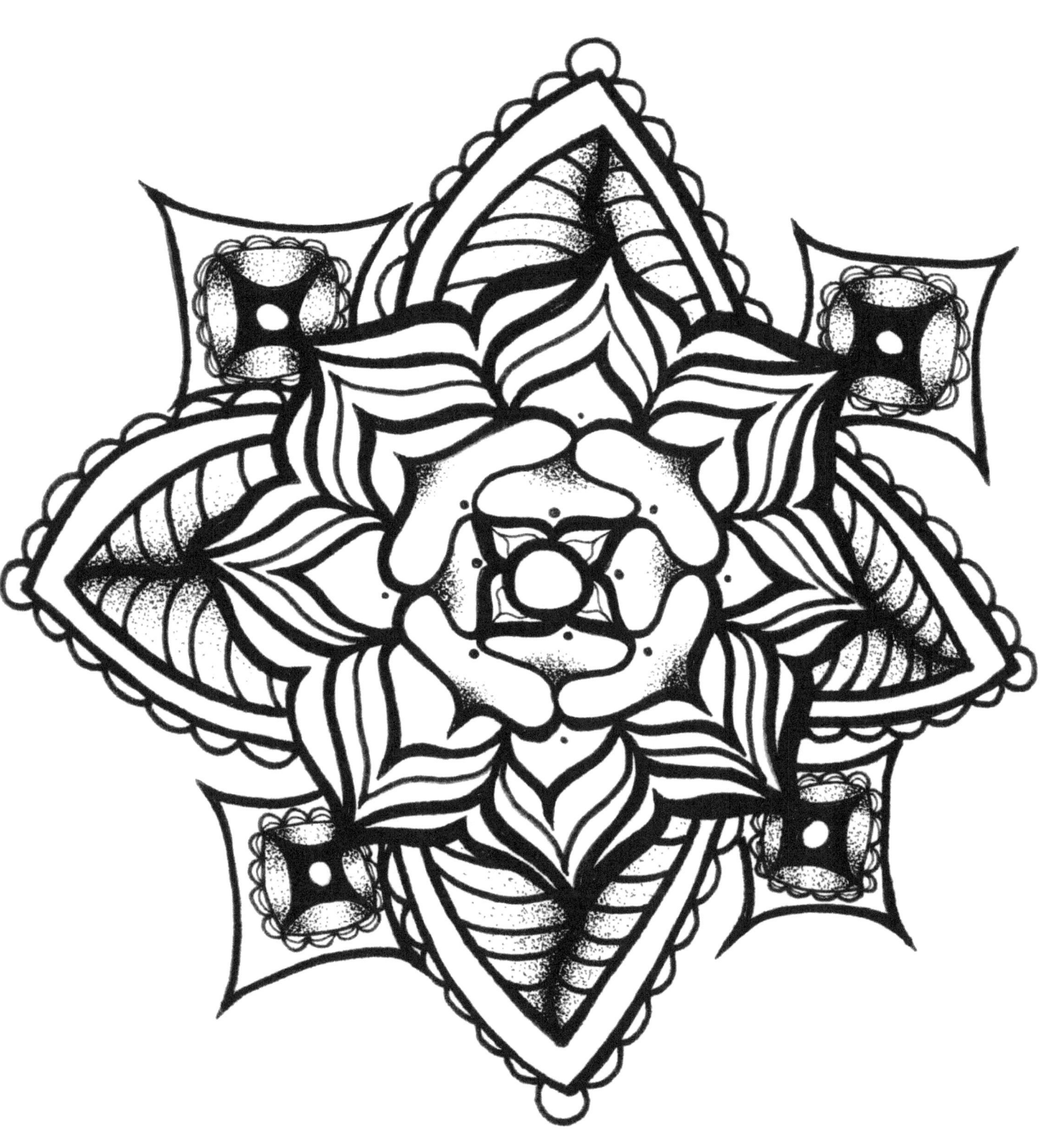

Colored by:

_____

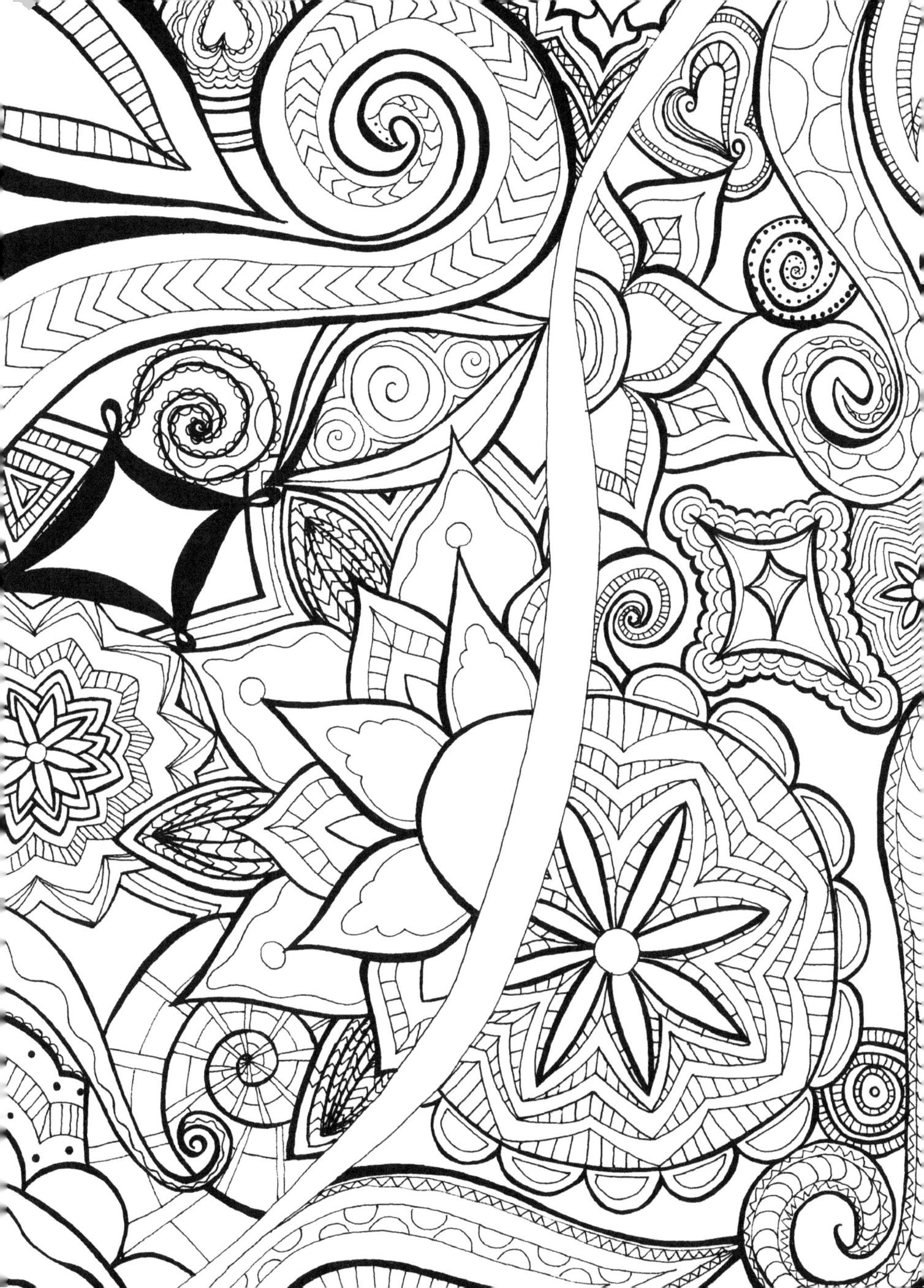

Colored by:

_____

SarahMe Doodles
by Sarah K. Presslor

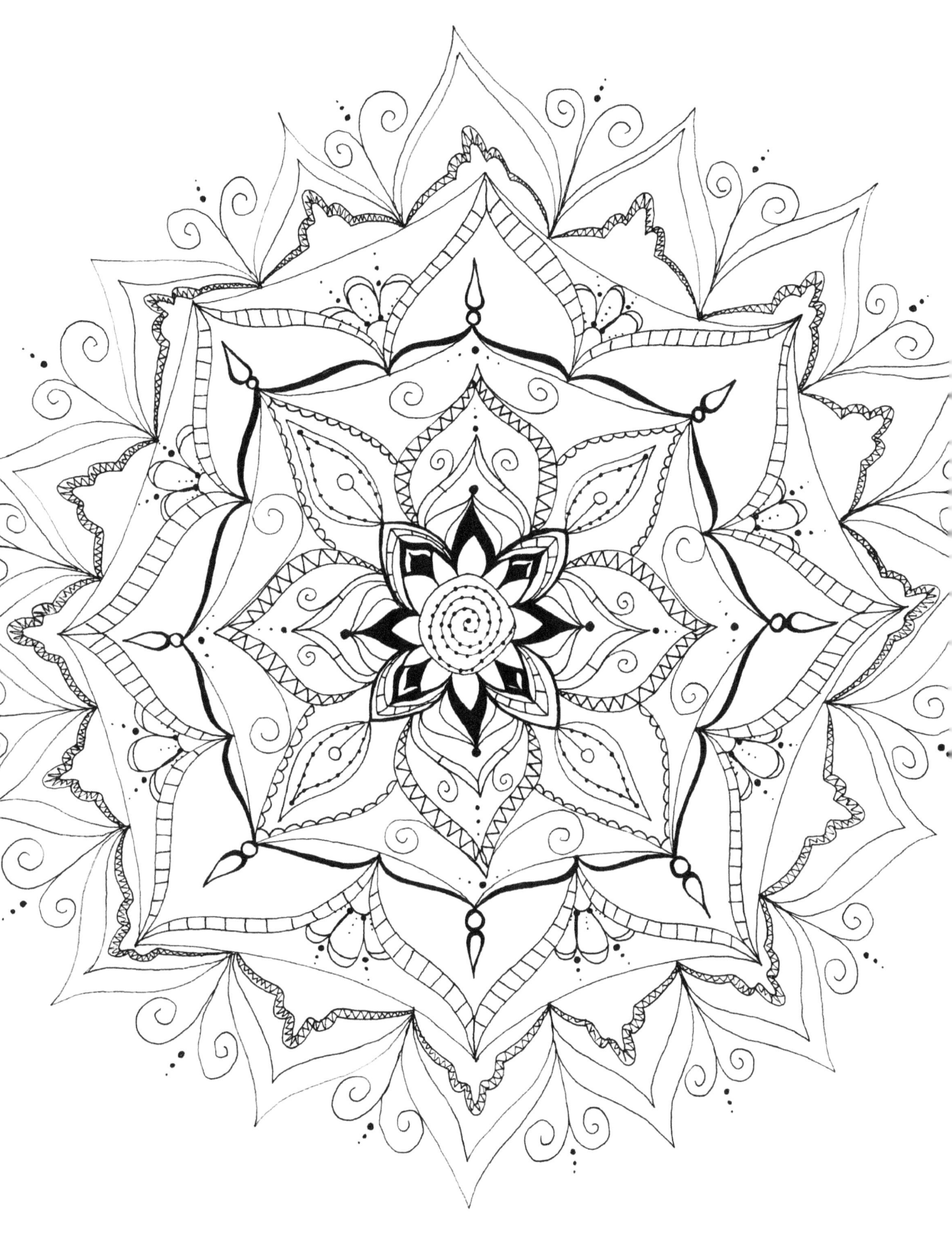

Colored by:

_____

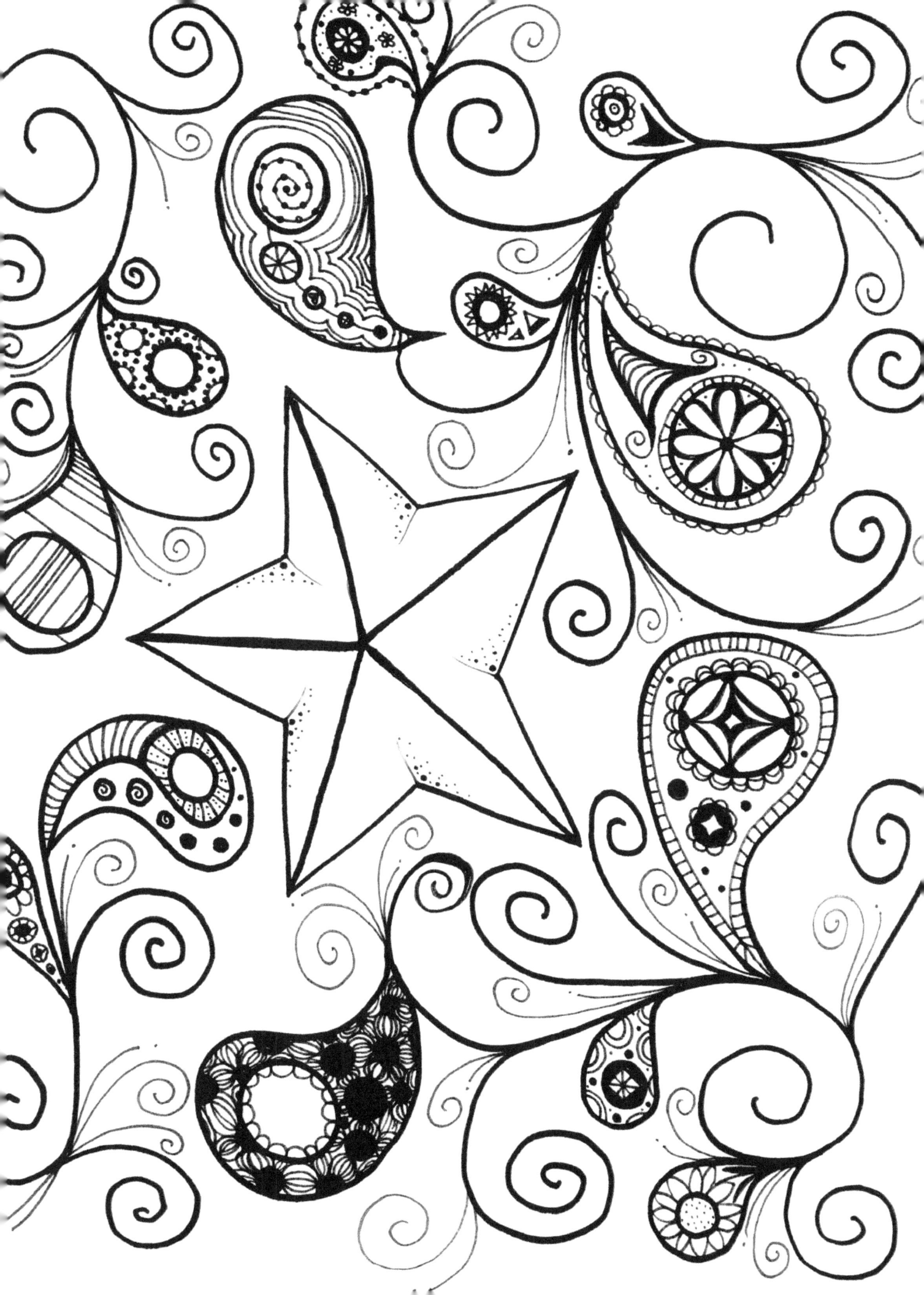

Colored by:

_____

SarahMe Doodles

by Sarah K. Presslor

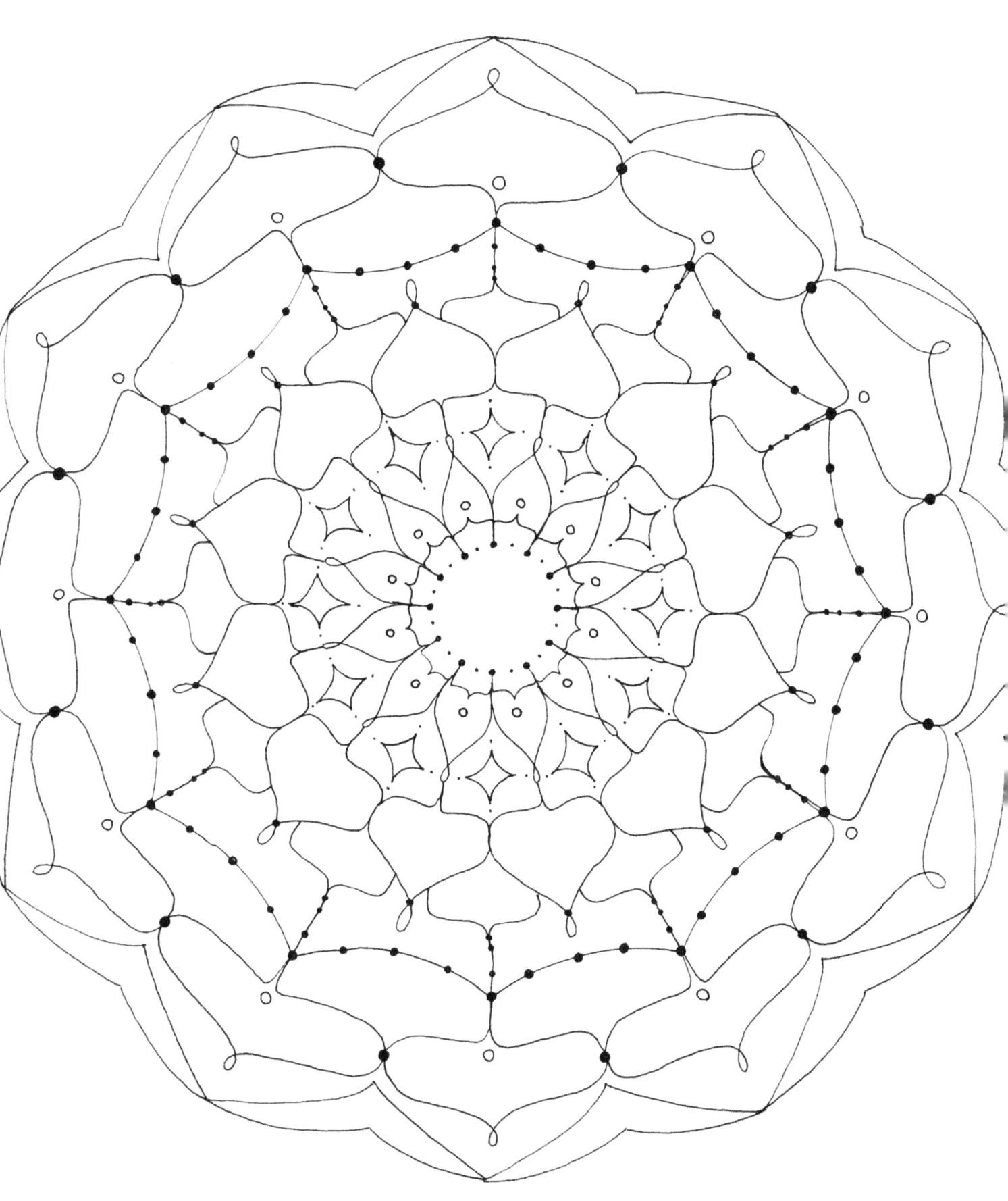

Colored by:

_____

SarahMe Doodles

by Sarah K. Presslor

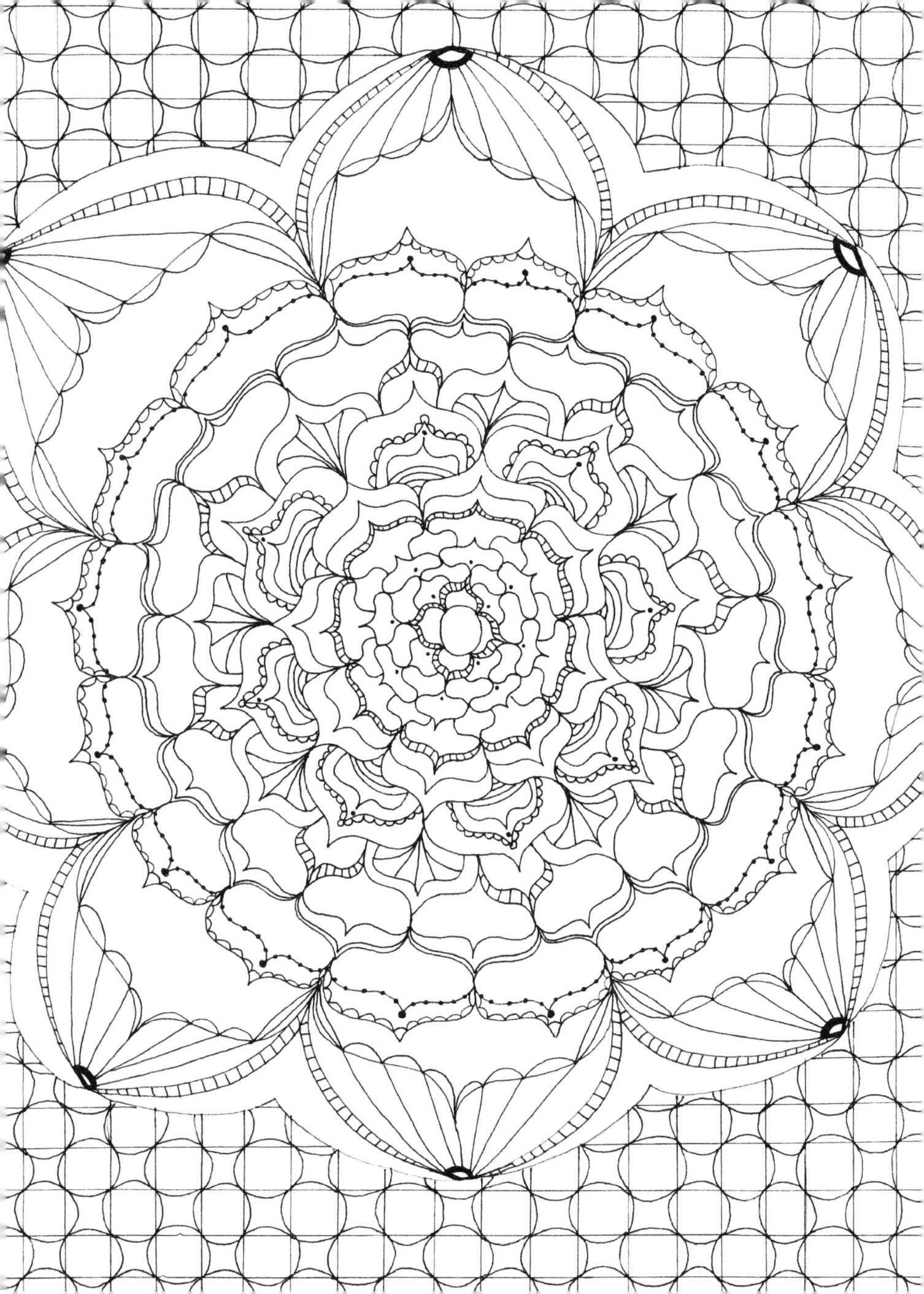

Colored by:

_____

SarahMe Doodles

by Sarah K. Presslor

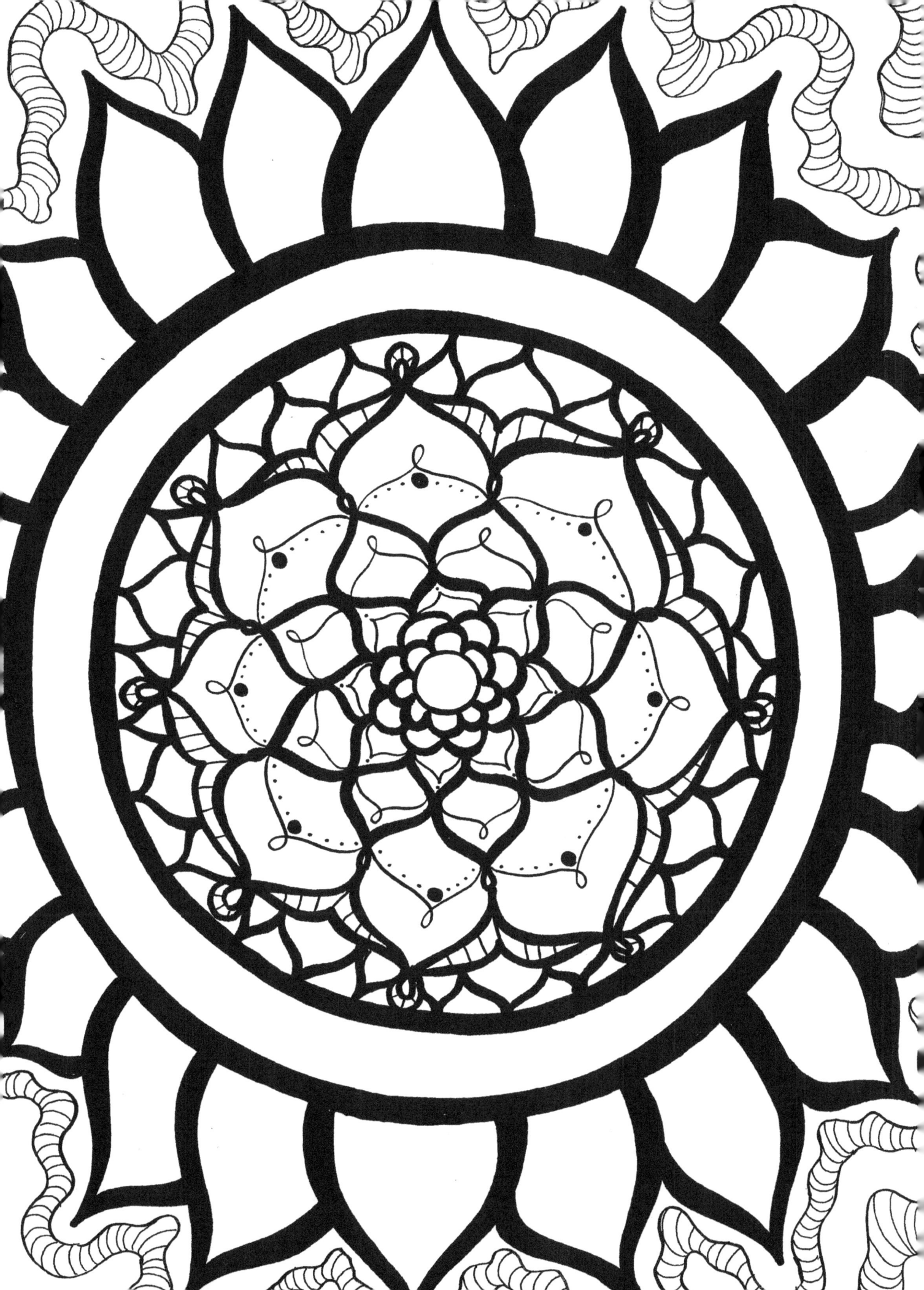

Colored by:

_____

SarahMe Doodles

by Sarah K. Presslor

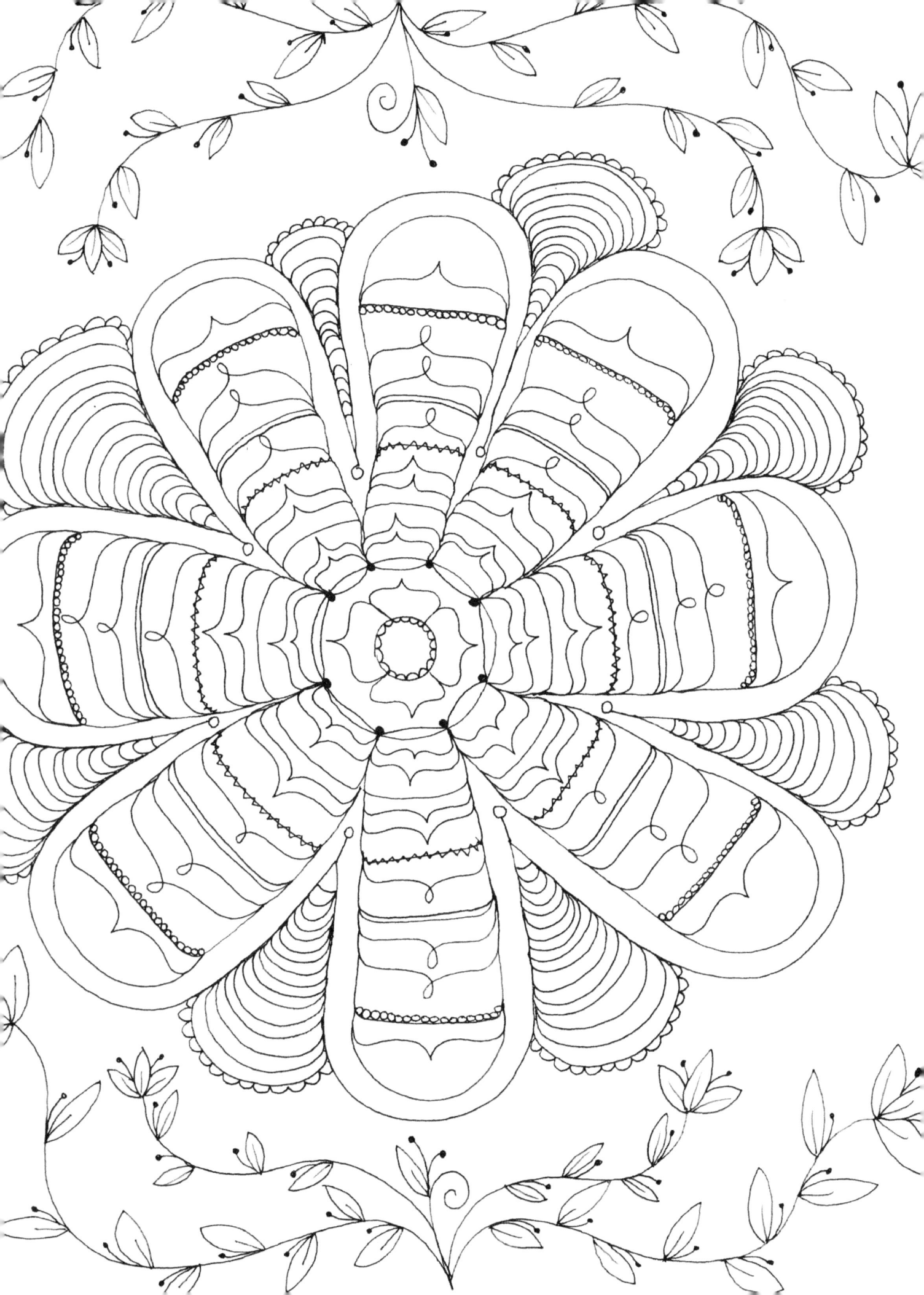

Colored by:

_____

SarahMe Doodles

by Sarah K. Presslor

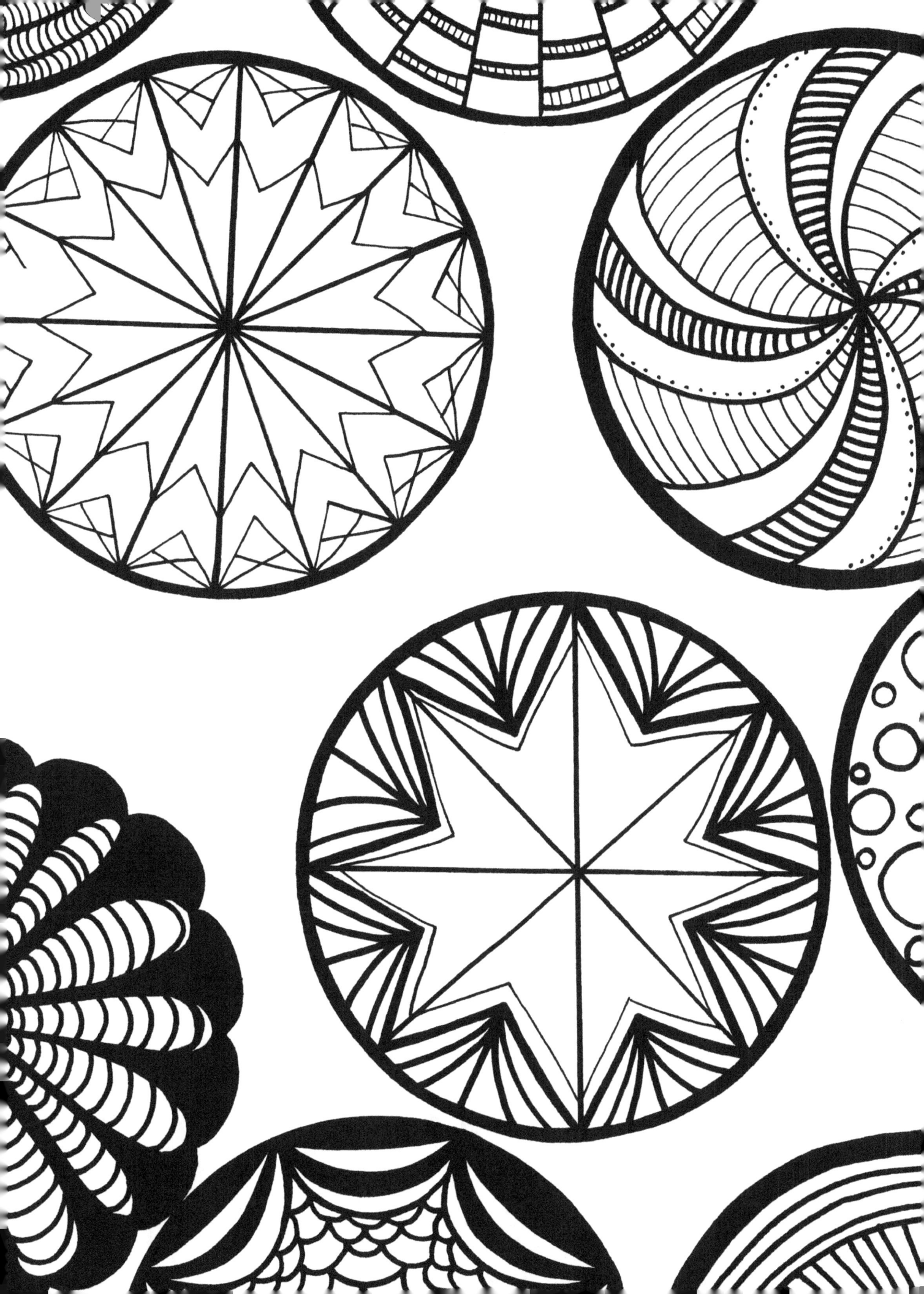

Colored by:

_____

SarahMe Doodles

by Sarah K. Presslor

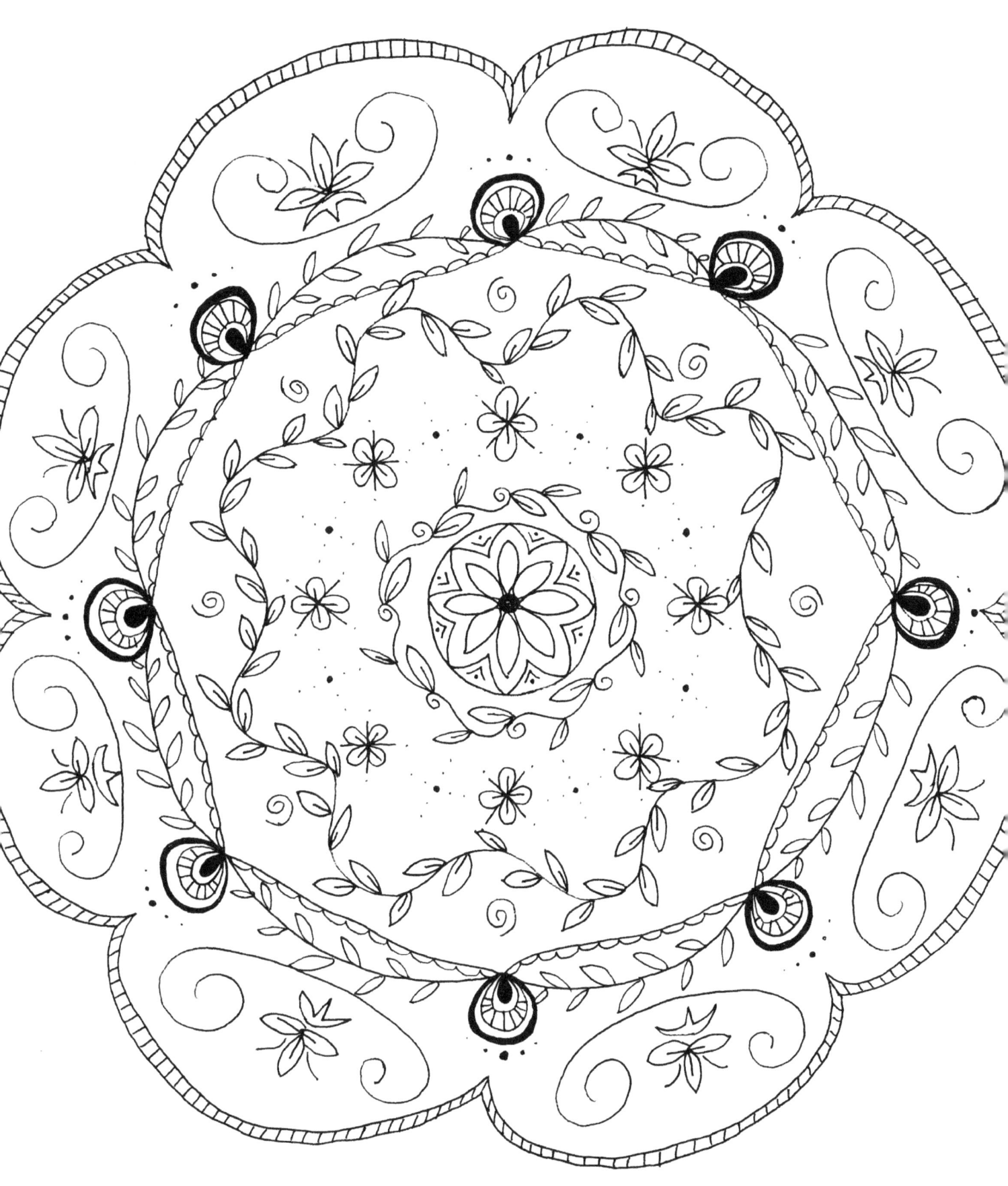

Colored by:

_____

SarahMe Doodles
by Sarah K. Presslor

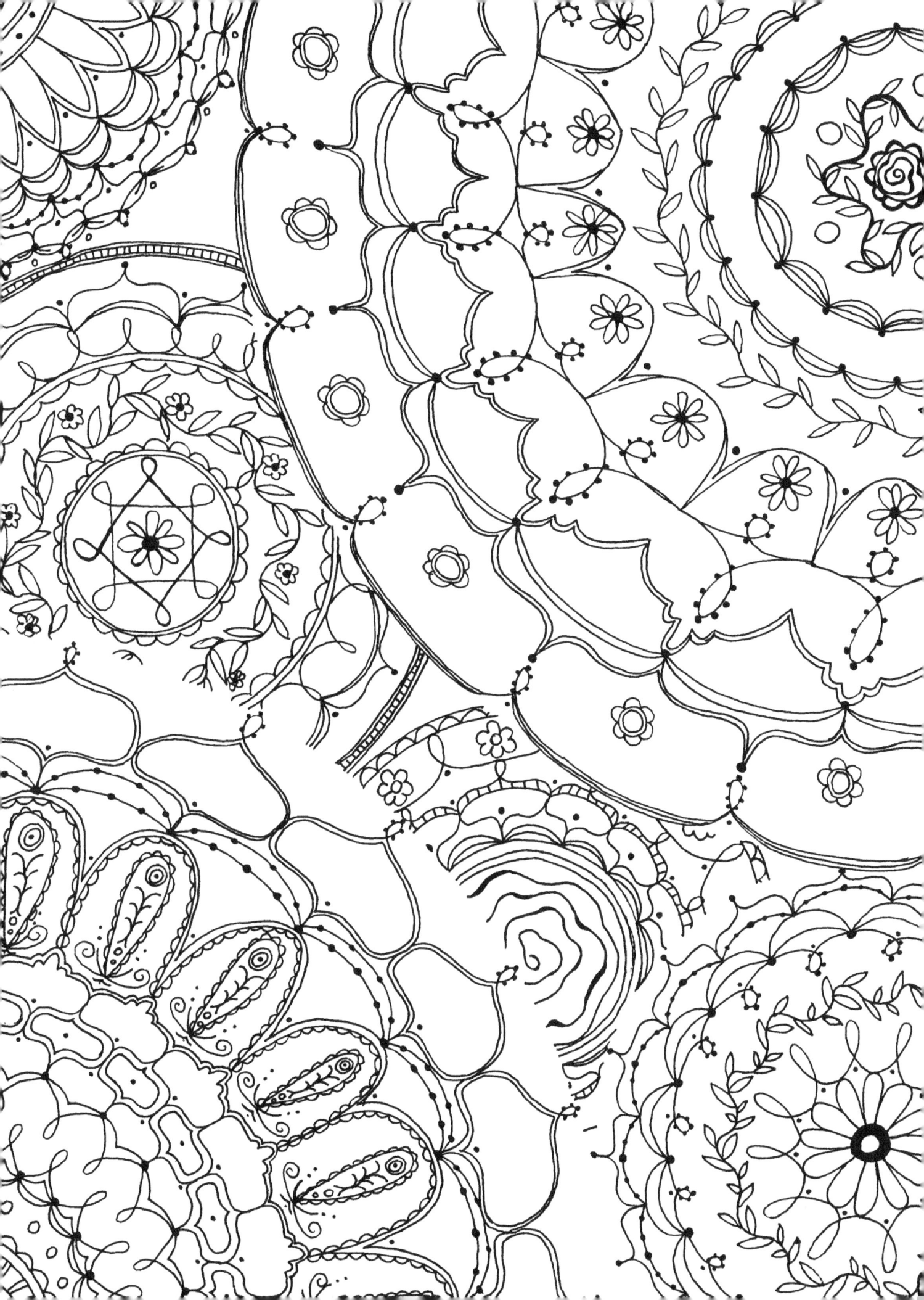

Colored by:

_____

www.ingramcontent.com/pod-product-compliance
Lightning Source LLC
Chambersburg PA
CBHW080631190526
45169CB00009B/3362